The Dumb Cops Volume 2

By William John Cranda

I dedicated this book to my loving wife who is not only my inspiration but the rock that my foundation is built on. Alice gives me strength to pursue what many would consider unachievable. If it was not for the loving care and devotion that Alice expresses my success would actually be failure.

I love my wife more than you could ever imagine she is the best thing that ever happened in my life.

My journey began in Miami, Florida on February 5, 2022. I flew out of Miami International Airport thanks from the help of Northeast Angel Flight.

The plane landed in Boston, Massachusetts on February 5, 2022 at 6:00 PM EST after being confined at assisted living in Miami.

I was forced to lay over in Boston, Massachusetts at the Boston, Massachusetts Hilton until 9:00 AM EST when I picked up my ride on a Concorde bus into Bangor, Maine. I didn't realize at the time of my departure that I was positive for the COVID-19 virus.

I was now subjected to the COVID-19 illness which created issues when I landed at the Bangor, Maine Concorde Bus lines terminal on February 6, 2022.

I collapsed right on the floor inside the bus terminal. I was rushed by ambulance to seek medical attention.

I was immediately rushed to the Northern Lights Eastern Maine Medical Center.

Where the incompetent staff began their journey of neglect which is just the normal display of incompetency of the authority at that hospital.

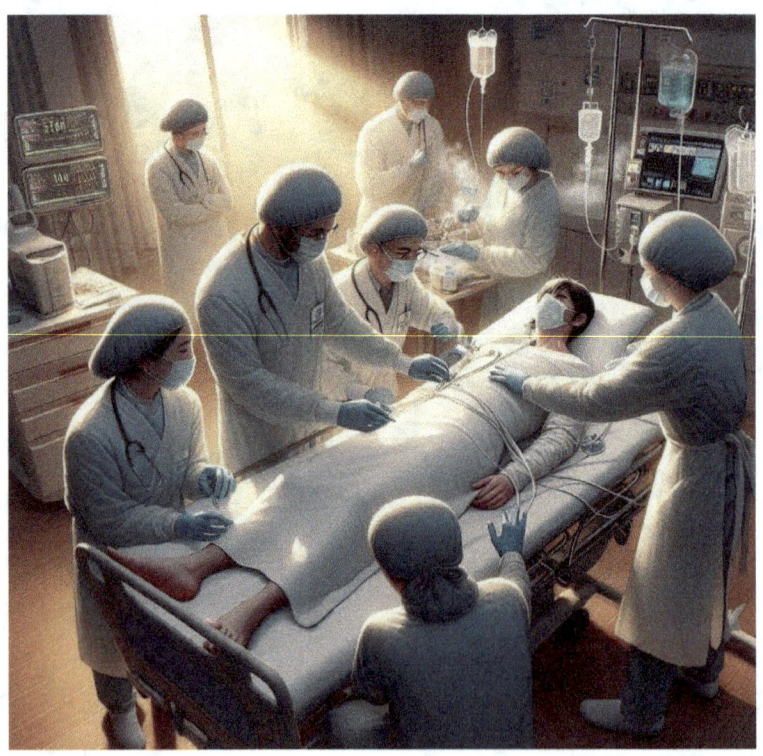

I was kept 24 hours not being capable of even carrying my 2 bags of clothes, being homeless upon my arrival back into the State of Maine.

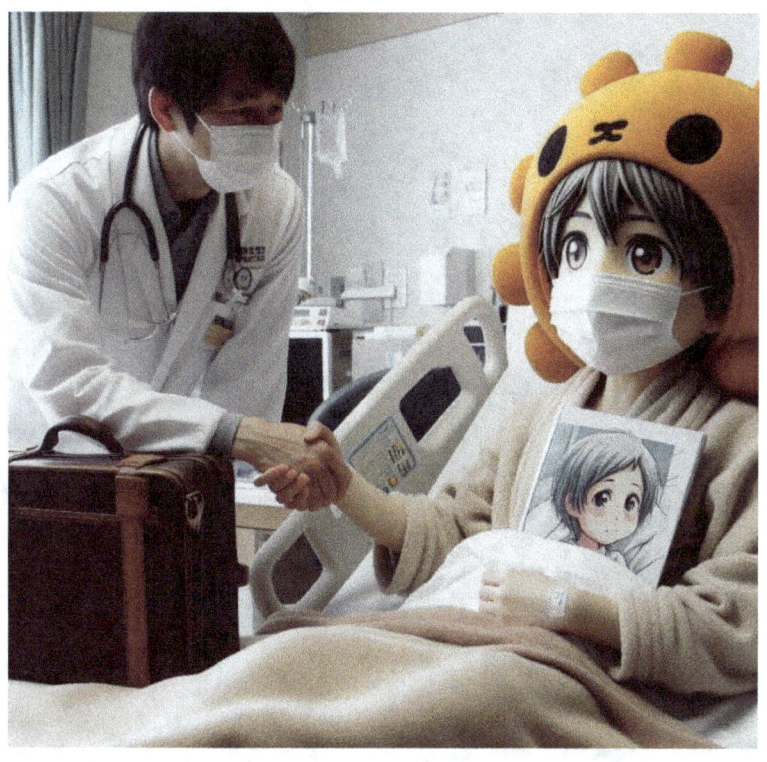

Upon my return to the State of Maine I was cast into homelessness barely capable of carrying the 2 bags of clothes that I had.

I was presented with an option by the Hope House Shelter of remaining in residence for the short-term.

I was forcibly thrown by law enforcement from the hospital to fend for myself on the street.

Being thrown from the hospital by their incompetent staff I was forced to start my plight into homelessness after Acadia Psychiatric Hospital denied my admission due to suicidal thoughts.

I was forced out into the cold with just two bags of clothes.

I was fortunate to meet Bruce and Donna of the Hope House Shelter in Bangor, Maine who gave me an option of living at the Hope House Shelter for the short-term.

I had to remain in quarantine at the Bangor, Maine Ramada Inn in Bangor, Maine until I was no longer COVID-19 symptomatic on March 1, 2022.

I was taken by a van after quarantine to the Hope House Shelter.

I only had 2 bags of clothes and nothing else for any of my possessions.

I was placed in dormitory one at the Hope House Shelter where I was given meals, a clean shower and social services.

I had to live each day with one eye open to prevent my personal belongings from being stolen from the thieves inside.

On March 28, 2022 my cell phone was stolen from dormitory 1 and I was informed that the

shelter was not responsible for stolen property.

I was temporarily separated from my wife because I didn't have phone privileges to be in touch with her.

April 1, 2022 I began my journey into independent living when Sue offered me a unit in transitional housing.

Transitional housing was nothing more than a stepping stone into the realm of independent living.

I made my friend Antonio who helped me out along the way by buying everything that I had that was not clothing related.

I began school on August 29, 2024 at Southern New Hampshire University in

Business Administration and Management Forensic Accounting.

I had my second phone stolen right from the dinner table in transitional housing totaling my losses at the Hope House Shelter in excess of $3787 dollars.

While at the Hope House Shelter I was subjected to the deceptive practices of the Penobscot Community Health and Counseling social worker.

Lauren Gregory who misrepresented the bankruptcy they talked me into filing.

While at the Hope House Shelter I also saw a quack psychiatrist Dr. Houlihan and malpracticing primary care doctor Jay Boardway who fraudulently got the social security administration and a representative payee involved because they didn't like my wife.

Dr. Houlihan and mal-practicing primary care doctor Jay Boardway got the social security administration to fraudulently administer a representative payee and denied my own wife control of my money.

The Social Security Administration uses strong armed tactics to deprive law abiding citizens of their sworn legal rights by the use of what they call a representative payee who is not even as qualified as I am with my credentials.

The Social Security Administration representative payee cannot even keep my debts out of collections because the debt collectors are knocking down my door.

The time has come and fall upon us it's time for the annual Thanksgiving dinner of turkey, cranberry sauce, potatoes, corn and stuffing.

I passed my first term classes of the year with a 4.0 GPA at Southern New Hampshire University.

I made the President List at Southern New Hampshire University and was honored by Senator Beldacci.

Classes are going good but I am not getting any sleep putting out reports and PowerPoint.

I worked really hard to achieve all my grades in forensic accounting a 4.0 GPA average.

Most of the time I am in front of the computer researching for my classes 4 weeks in advance.

Christmas came and another lonely dinner spent by myself all alone.

The winter has come and second term is done I made it to the President's store again this time being inducted into the National Society of Leadership and Success.

Things were not all that bad on the transition side of the shelter it was a good meal.

The shelter was also kind with health in mind to provide a shower or a bath.

The winter turned out cold, rainy, and snowy the weather even brought a blizzard.

The night was never dull in transitional because we watched television or played board games.

Winters dreary skies broke to weather by no surprise to bring the May flowers to bloom before your very eyes.

Antonio was really kind he even let me borrow his motorized scooter to go to Walmart for some groceries.

I rode the commuter into Bangor, Maine to do some more shopping for miscellaneous supplies.

Passing time was never a challenge because I bought myself a drone so I spent my time flying it to make my summer more fun.

Alice Kate Crandall is still going to school in the military to get a degree in combat technology God only knows when she will be finished.

Being in the military is supposed to be honorable and with respect but it's just a bunch of foolishness and dreck.

Alice is a officer combat specialist in the Army, however through past family experience the military like the Social Security Administration only destroys the lives of those who serve their country.

When we examine police corruption in the State of Maine we begin with the most corrupt agency in the entire Penobscot county Orono, Maine who uses strong hold tactics and coercing to achieve their goals.

I had a brief moment of psychiatric breakdown due to the failure of my medical team to prescribe my medication which the police now justify police intimidation.

The Orono police department violates your civil rights on a daily basis with warrantless searches and police investigations.

The Orono police department has continued ongoing harassment for law abiding citizens to instill fear of your very own life.

The police in Orono, Maine through continuing harassment are in violation of various statutes such as:

Title 18 U.S.C. 241

Title 18 U.S.C. 242

Title 5 Chapter 37

Federal 42 U.S C 1983

Title 34-B 3862

Title 34-B 3863

Title 17

Title 14 Chapter 747 8241

Finally the blatant disregard for the Civil Rights Act of 1871

The Orono, Maine police department violates your civil rights even by harassing you at 6:00 AM EST at the corner bus stop.

My problem with the corruption in the Orono police department began when Penobscot Community Health and Counseling withheld my psychiatric medication cold turkey for 3 weeks.

Due to the negligence and malpractice of Penobscot Community Health and Counseling I had a meltdown a total mental breakdown.

Due to circumstances beyond my control it now gives the Orono police department carte blanche continuing harassment at all hours of the day and night to come and harass me.

However, the corrupt Orono, Maine police department feels it necessary for continuing police brutality and intimidation.

The Orono police department bases their investigations on hearsay evidence and baseless innuendo.

The Orono Maine police department also continues to strip your rights by having you continually and baselessly hauled to the hospital and dehumanizing by countless numbers of useless strip searches.

The Orono Maine police department bases their investigations on word of mouth by people who are not even located within the state.

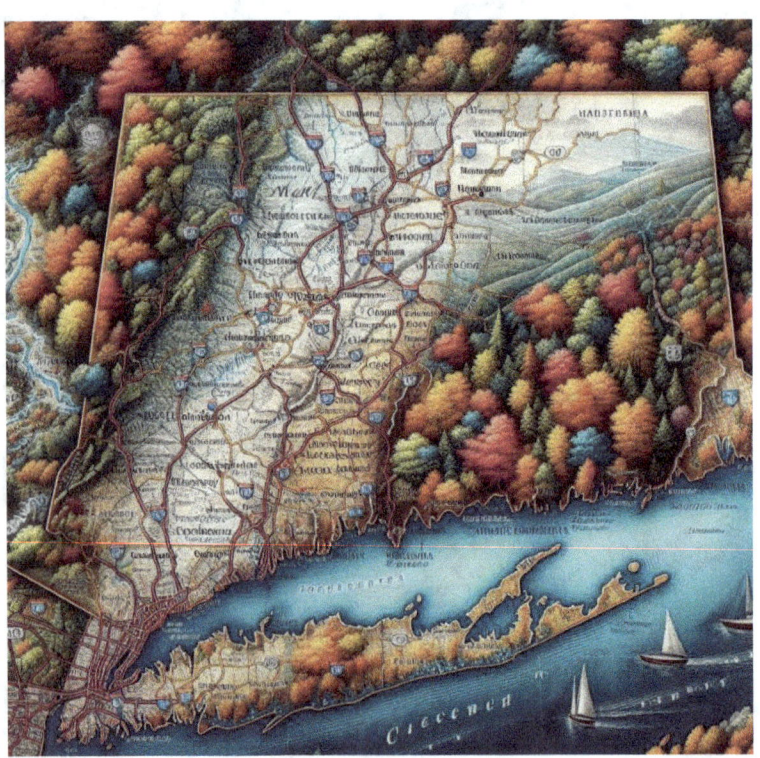

In Orono Maine it's even by needle, drug dealer pushing and even prostitution you can always count on their local law enforcement.

The Orono Maine police department doesn't even know how to follow up and investigation because they base their motives on baseless accusations and false representations

If the pompous windbag Orono Maine police department

were capable of a thorough investigation the idiots would have found out that the false representations came from those who are trying to control my money through greed and corruption.

It seems like all the Orono Maine police department does is create problems where none actually exist.

The uncaring and heartless nature of those sworn to protect us only jeopardizes public safety by violating a person's civil rights based on falsifying accusations by a greedy family.

The problem with my family is that they are greedy and corrupt and have plagued my wife and I with problems all over money because they are trying to get their hands on my assets.

Let's talk about the law and ethics is a ethical to base an investigation on hearsay evidence.

Is it ethical to persecute based on falsified evidence.

Is it ethical to persecute without corroboration.

Is it ethical to form investigations based on accusations from greedy grabbers

Is it ethical to base investigations without proper follow through.

The Orono Maine police department persecutes without substantiation.

When the abuse of power by the Orono Maine police department weighs against the rights of the law-abiding citizens justice is never done.

To be persecuted by the Orono Maine police department wrongfully and unsubstantiated leaves us no better than those persecuted Jesus on the cross.

William John Crandall, I lived in North Stonington Connecticut until I was 18 years old. I graduated high school from Ella Grasso Southeastern Technical High School in 1988 when I moved to Laramie, Wyoming to attend Heavy Equipment Technician School. I spent a year and a half on my friend Patrick Whitman ranch learning all I could about horses and pro-roping. I returned to the state of Maine after my Wyoming graduation to establish my own horse farm in Lincoln, Maine named Isfappaloosa Farms because I raised show Appaloosas. I unfortunately met with ill health requiring 13 back surgeries 2 of them total fusions to my spine. I took Civil and Environmental Engineering courses while undergoing surgery and I graduated with a 4.0 GPA. I now reside in Orono, Maine with my wife Alice Kate Crandall. I am working towards my master's degree in business administration and management at

Southern New Hampshire University while I continue to write my children's books.

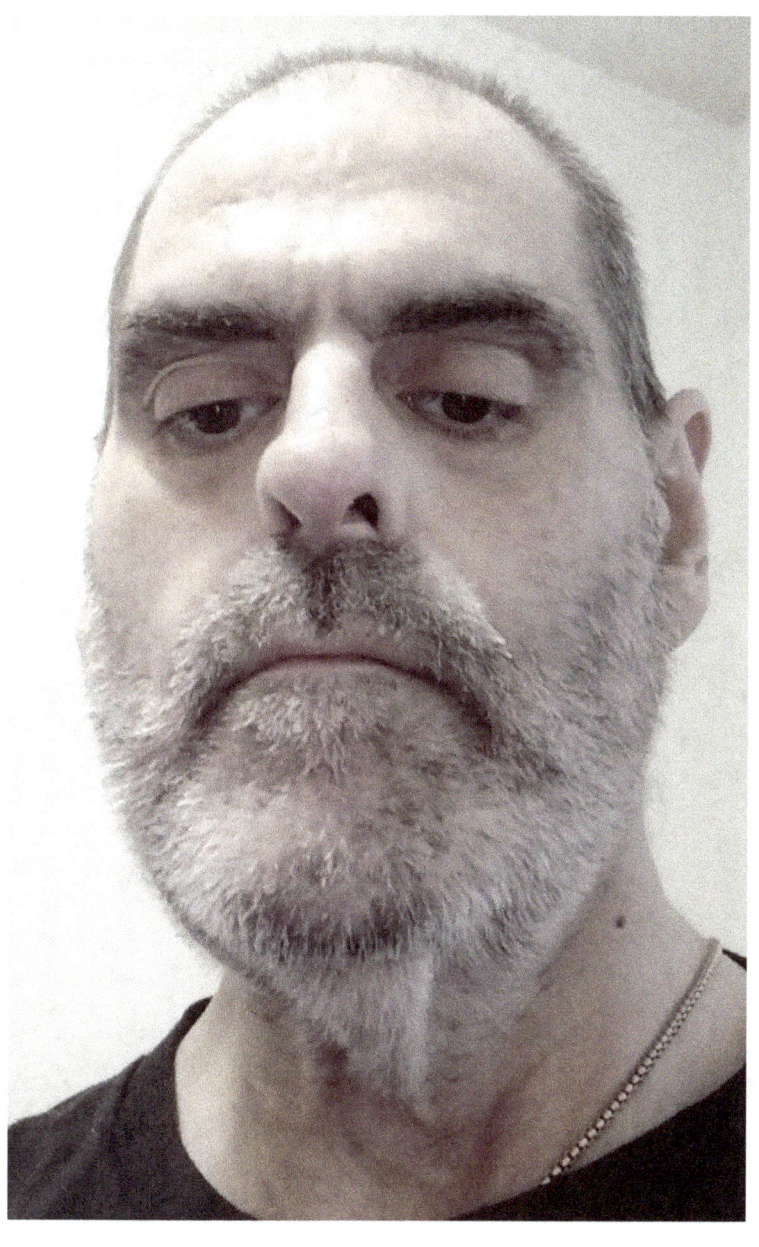

www.ingramcontent.com/pod-product-compliance
Lightning Source LLC
Chambersburg PA
CBHW071106240526
45469CB00006BD/2342